To

Kari

With Love

Elaine

Date

February, 2020

Thanks for sharing
God's love with the girls
on Wednesday evening!

THE LOVE BOOK

ANTHONY DeSTEFANO

HARVEST HOUSE PUBLISHERS
EUGENE, OREGON

THE LOVE BOOK

Text Copyright © 2015 Anthony DeStefano
Photos compiled by Anthony DeStefano

Published by Harvest House Publishers
Eugene, Oregon 97402
www.harvesthousepublishers.com

ISBN 978-0-7369-6473-9

Design and production by Left Coast Design

Photographs used with permission from the following sources:
istock Photo on pages: 5, 14, 16, 18, 24, 30, 31, 35, 45, 53, 59
Shutterstock on pages: 17, 22
Getty Images on pages: 28, 64
Dollar Photo Club on pages: 3, 4, 6, 7, 8, 9, 10, 11, 12, 13, 15, 19, 20, 21, 23, 24, 25, 26, 27, 29, 32, 33, 34, 36, 37, 38, 39, 40, 41, 42, 43, 44, 46, 47, 48, 49, 50, 51, 52, 54, 55, 56, 57, 58, 60, 61, 62, 63

Digital photo editing by Schmalen Design, Inc., Dahlonega, Georgia

Printed in China

15 16 17 18 19 20 21 22 23 / LP / 10 9 8 7 6 5 4 3 2 1

This book
is for my wife,

JORDAN

Everyone says that **LOVE** is the key to happiness.

But if that's true...

why are there so many unhappy people in the world?

After all, there are thousands of books, poems, movies, and songs about love—you would think everyone would be an expert by now.

But they're not. In fact, love is probably the most abused, confused, and misused word in the English language. People just don't seem to get it.

And can you blame them?
Love does such crazy things to you
it makes your head spin!

It can make the whole world sunny,
no matter what the weather.

It can literally make
your hair stand up
from excitement.

But it can also
make your stomach
do somersaults.

It can make you abnormally obsessive

and want to
show off all
your talents...

and care about how you look much
more than you ever did before.

But it can also make you jealous for no reason...

and absolutely ruin your
judgment and your vision.

Love can make you braver than you
ever thought you could be...

but also
more afraid.

I've tried to understand love, but I've been
baffled and hurt by it more often than not. In fact,
over the years I've been beaten up pretty badly.

I've had my heart broken into a million little pieces by cruel people.

I've been disappointed by
my family and friends.

I've learned the hard way what love is NOT. It's not just a feeling because feelings go up and down like a roller coaster—and you can't base your happiness on what amounts to a ride.

It's not just being infatuated because
sometimes infatuation can get you
into a boatload of trouble.

It's not just being romantic because
sometimes the most loving thing you can
do for someone is very UNromantic.

It's not just being soft and mushy and sentimental and kind because—let's face it—sometimes tough love is the only thing that works. Sometimes you just have to let people experience a little pain in order to grow.

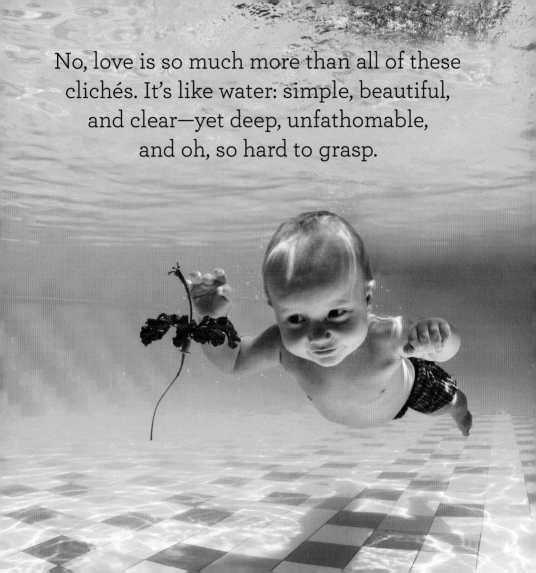

No, love is so much more than all of these
clichés. It's like water: simple, beautiful,
and clear—yet deep, unfathomable,
and oh, so hard to grasp.

But there must be a key to understanding love. There must be a key that unlocks love's great mystery.

And if such a key does exist, what can it look like? It doesn't look like a heart—despite what the greeting card companies tell us—

or like cupid's bow and arrow

or like a bouquet of flowers—
though that can be nice—

or like chocolate—though
that can be even nicer—

or even jewelry—though that can be nicer still!

God is Love

No, none of these things is the key to love.
I may not be the most spiritual person in the
world, but I know the Bible says that God *is*
love. Hearts and flowers and chocolate and
jewelry are all wonderful, but they
can't be equal to God.

When all is said and done, do you know
what the key to love looks most like?

A cross.

Yes, a cross. True love means self-sacrifice. It means giving, giving, and giving some more—until you've given absolutely everything.

It means loving the way God loves us—without limit. It means saying: This is my body, *given up for you.*

True love bears all things, endures all things,
and suffers all things. It doesn't count
any costs or look for any rewards.

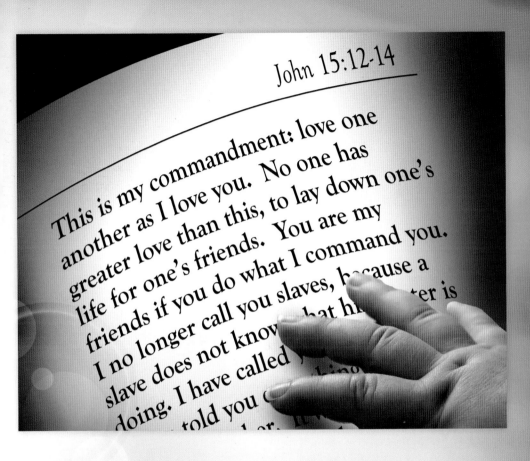

John 15:12-14

This is my commandment: love one another as I love you. No one has greater love than this, to lay down one's life for one's friends. You are my friends if you do what I command you. I no longer call you slaves, because a slave does not know what his ter is doing. I have called told you

True love always does what's best for the *other* person.

When you love like that, then you become the
kind of person you were *created* to be—and
what you experience as a result is much
deeper than any mere pleasure. It's *joy*.

But practicing true love isn't easy!
In fact, it's the hardest thing in the
world. It means sacrificing every
bit of yourself for your family...

and your country...

and your faith.

It means loving yourself despite all your weaknesses and faults and insecurities—but loving yourself *so much* that you challenge yourself to be the best person you can be physically, mentally, emotionally, and spiritually.

It means surrendering all that you have
and all that you are for that one special
person who is the *love of your life*.

It doesn't matter if they're rich or poor...

young or old,

healthy or sick.

It doesn't matter if they've lost their hearing...

or their slender figure.

It doesn't matter if they're irritating...

or grumpy...

or ungrateful.

True love means being willing to give every last drop of blood for that person—no matter what the circumstance, no matter what the cost—unconditionally and *forever*.

It's a *decision* that transcends all human
feeling and understanding and makes it
possible to overcome every obstacle
and weather every storm,

a decision that gives you freedom. Yes, that's the meaning of true love and nothing else.

That's the key to understanding
the great mystery of life.

That's the key to finding happiness
in this world full of suffering.

That's the key to finding happiness
in this world full of suffering.

And THAT, by the way…

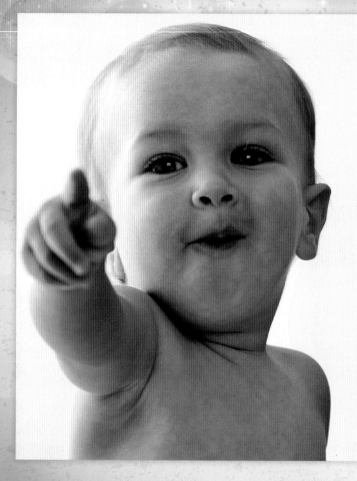

...is how I love YOU!